Not really, but I'm sure if whale sharks could digest chocolate they probably would love it too! This title references a view on describing people as flavors. I've always thought of ways to create acts of kindness and how in the United States peoples' identity is predominately described by race. Would it not be kind if we could all reference self by complexion and by a flavor? If that were the case, I would be considered Chocolate. So, this title uses the word Chocolate to describe my flavor, which to some is my complexion, and others my race.

This book is really about the affection I have for the whale sharks, their gentle spirits and how swimming with them has helped me heal from my only child's tragic death from suicide. Because Whale Sharks are in the shark family a lot of people elude to it as being dangerous. Even I was guilty of that perception.

My hopes in sharing my journey is to help others see that while there are situations and things in life that appear or have the perception of being large and overwhelming, like the whale sharks, there is a potential lesson in all situations to help strengthen the spirit. Bringing with it consciousness and kindness to the universe.

Namaste,
Gina M. Smallwood

During the winter of 2011, my employer decided to give staff the gift of time, an entire week off from Christmas through the New Year. Although, I would have loved to travel away to the sea, gulf or the ocean, I did not have the resources to take a last minute vacation. So, I opted instead to go to "Sacred Moon" our country home purchased to operate a healing space in Fairburn, Georgia. Although, I had taken residence in Georgia in 2007, I had never visited the Georgia Aquarium, so I decided I would visit it during my Christmas break. I jokingly said to a colleague, it would be nice if they let you swim with the fish. Lord and behold, five minutes later the universe guided me to the internet and I had booked the last spot for a swim on Christmas day with the Whale Sharks (the largest fish) affectionately known as the "Gentle Giants". Up until that time, I was not familiar with Whale Sharks like I was with Dolphins, which I swam with in Jamaica and Curacao. I remember being so excited, and sharing it with my sister who said "That's for Chicks (expletive) who have everything."

Christmastime, since my son Kelvin's transition, was a very painful time of year. So this present to swim with the Gentle Giants was a way I could honor my son's spirit (who was a scuba diver) and embark on an adventure I know he would enjoy. It was only a week away, but I was so excited I could hardly contain myself. Finally, it was Christmas Eve and I remembered slight fear surfacing on what I was about to embark. I started thinking what if I don't have enough stamina to stay in the water? Will there be life jackets? The funny part is that I never thought about them biting or attacking me. I got down on my knees and prayed for safety, went to bed early and the rest I left to God.

The swim I encountered on December 25, 2011 changed my life and took my breath away. Literally! It was the most spiritual experience I had encountered. I had become one with the Gentle Giants and my son's spirit. The swim in Georgia included three whale sharks, four manta rays, and about 48 other schools of fish. You become a fish for at least 45 minutes that you're in the aquarium. Depending on the gear you use (scuba or snorkeling) your breath becomes very shallow. I remember after the swim asking the instructors if there were any jobs available at the aquarium. Life could be that simple, swimming with Whale Sharks every day. I purchased the video footage of my swim and this photo to share with family and friends who know I can be quite eccentric when it comes to affection for the unorthodox, like the Gentle Giants.

Here is what I learned about the "Gentle Giants." The Whale Shark, (Rhincodon typus) is the largest living species of fish and the worlds largest shark. The shark is primarily grey in color with a white underside. Whale Sharks primarily live in tropical warm waters and are generally found in the open ocean. With a mouth up to 5 feet wide and 300 rows of tiny teeth (up to 3,000 teeth) they can seem intimidating. The Whale Shark is estimated to live somewhere between 60 and 150 years and is believed to reach sexual maturity around 30 years. Whale Sharks have been recorded to be up to 46 feet weighing up to 15 tons. The average Whale Shark is around 25 feet long. The Whale Shark is a filter feeder. It feeds on phytoplankton, macro-algae, plankton, krill and small nektonic life, such as small squid or vertebrates. This species, despite its enormous size, does not pose any significant danger to humans. This is another reason that the phenomenal gathering of large numbers near Isla Holbox, Mexico, parts of Australia, and the Philippines is an event to be seen and respected. Whale sharks are listed as vulnerable on the IUCN (International Union for Conservation of Nature) Red List of Threatened Species.

So two years later in March 2013, I was contemplating what I might do for Mother's day, yet another painful holiday. I stumbled on a Groupon for a hotel in Isla Holbox (meaning the "Blackhole" in Yucatec Mayan), Quintana Roo Mexico in the Yucatan Peninsula. I had never heard of the Island and decided to do some research and what did I find? The Gentle Giants! Whale Sharks migrate there every year for about three and half months. I was overdue for a vacation and had decided I would treat myself for Mother's Day. The only glitch, they only migrate from June to mid-September. So I decided to treat myself to a trip for my birthday to Isla Holbox to swim with the Gentle Giants. I was so excited for nearly four months, I hardly could contain myself. I purchased everything I needed for the trip and even brushed up on my swimming.

Then the time arrived, I had arranged an eight-day trip (August 14-21, 2013) that included three days of traveling. Isla Holbox is a two and a half to three hour drive north of Cancun, Mexico. Then you have to catch a half hour ferry to this remote charming little island. I was flying out on a Wednesday, so after work Tuesday night before my trip, I checked the weather. Oh no ($#!+)! There is a rain forecast for my entire trip, all but the day I was scheduled to arrive. So my angst was whether the rainy weather would prevent my swim with the whale sharks in their natural habitat, as I had so longed to do. After talking to my big sister, she reminded me that storms come and go. I was reassured that what I had set out to do, God was opening up the universe to make it happen. I never imagined just how exciting the entire journey would manifest itself to be.

Get Ready
Get Set
Here We Go!

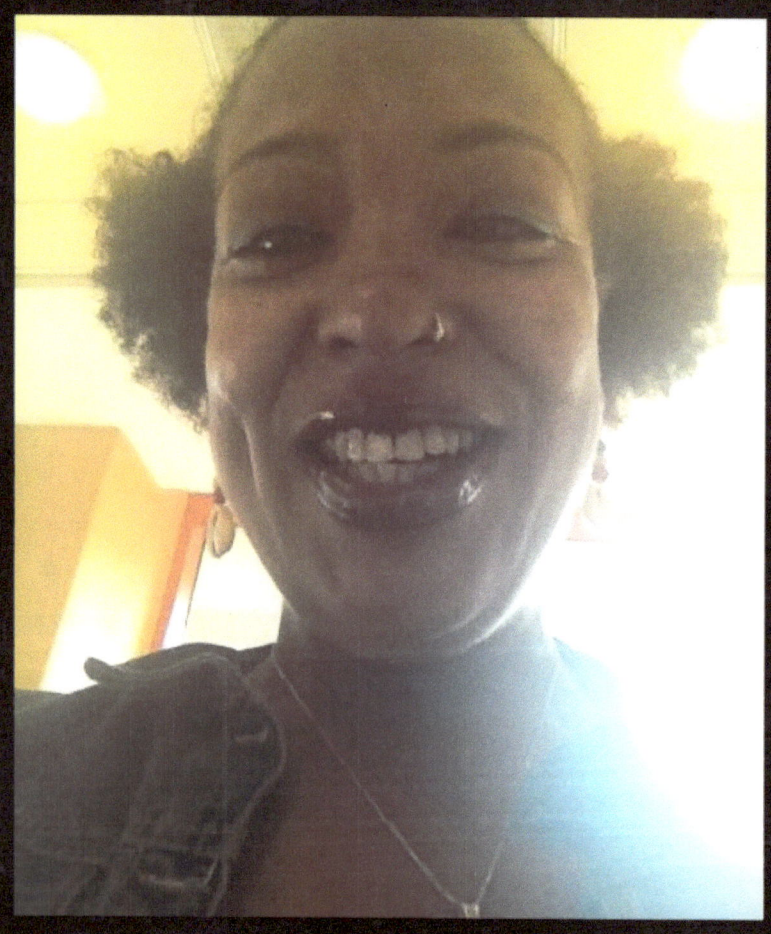

As the Universe opened the door,

my heart followed..........

By Land, Air, Land and Sea
"Gentle Giants" Chocolate is here!
Destination: Isla Holbox, Mexico
Wednesday – August 14, 2013

By the time I had arrived to Isla Holbox, I had been up and running for 12 hours (one and half hours before leaving home, one hour traveling to the airport, two hours check in, three and half hour flight, three and half hour drive and a half hour ferry ride). From the air I shot a photo, which I believe to be Isla Holbox.

During the road trip, I saw Mexico's military, ten little townships, mucho ranchos, and then my driver was pulled over for speeding.

We were held at a police checkpoint for almost 45 minutes. They took her driver's license because she did not have cash at the checkpoint. Her fine was $50. If she paid it within 48 hours it would be $25 and she would get her license back.

Thought: What if the police did that in the USA?

While at the checkpoint my driver got out of the car and for 15 minutes I could not see her or the police.

Thought: Oh hell, I am in Mexico! What if they pop the trunk and somehow drugs were planted in my luggage or the driver I hired online was a drug smuggler?

Now you see why I am cheesing so hard.

Great Room Amenities

Direct Door Sign (Come In/Go Away)
Frogs
Comfortable bed
Hearts on the wall
Bottle caps for your contact lenses
Adopted Dog
Conscious effort to save the planet

Priorities: Contact Case, which you need every day because you wear contacts or eyelashes, which you never wear?

"Oh $#!+" Probably the most used expression on the planet and this part of the journey., Especially every time I would forget and flush toilet tissue.

Chow Down/Local Eats

Great Paladar!

Most times I wonder?

Le Jardin French bakery – Great Breakfast! Three days in a row!

Best damn hand-made ceviche! Chef Leonardo

Tasty local food joints. I must say the food was pleasant, but the best food I've tasted in the world is in Italy!

Rainy Thursday

Anticipation

When you plan for something to happen with the greatest of intentions and you want the plans to work out in your favor.
Ugh!
Tropical Rain=Variables

Half the day was spent testing the Ipad waterproof case I purchased. How about the Ebay seller sent me the wrong case? No underwater photos? Not! When all else fails you find a replacement like a disposable underwater camera.

Did I mention, I polished my nails 4 times?

"TGIF"

Isla Holbox Apartments for sale: Any Buyers?

"Rain, Rain Go Away" I'm starting not to like you, not another bloody day!

Gondola or Rain Boots? No, flip flops or barefoot.
Walking through the flooded streets of Isla Holbox for 4 days is not for the faint at heart.
#monsoons
Daily Mantra: $#!+ I'm a survivor, I'm not going to give up. I'm going to swim with them whale sharks!

"TGIF"

There's the sun (son) peeking out of the clouds. Part of life's ebbs and flows.

Smiling cause I just received an email, subject: Your trip is being paid for. Hallelujah!

"Swim at your own risk" not once did I see a lifeguard.

Fly Fishing Anyone?

Friday was the scheduled day to swim with the Whale Sharks. Forecast: No possible swim until Monday or Tuesday if it doesn't rain again. The "Gentle Giants" have gone under and we have to relocate them. #noworries

While sitting at a bar on the beach, I met two beautiful spirits from Australia (Giselle and Shellie) who are scuba divers that swam with the whale sharks and had been in Mexico for a few weeks. They were about to have dinner and invited me to join them. We spent hours eating, laughing and crying, As we shared our victory stories as women,

Benefits of new friends
#place2stayinAustralia
#AustraliaHasGentleGiants

We also shared stories about were we reside on the planet. I learned Koala bears die in forest fires because they are so tired after eating eucalyptus, they sleep though the fire. I learned Kangaroos are a nuisance in Australia like deer are in the USA. I learned Kangaroo fighting can be amusing.

What I learned the most from this exchange is no matter where we come from, as women, we are united.

Friday's Moon over Isla Holbox

"Saturday's View"
Isla Holbox from a Lounger
'Blue Skies looking at me, nothing but blue skies do I see.'

Today while snorkeling, in the distance there were three dolphins, then something touched my leg and I shot out of the water like a flying fish.

"Saturday's Sunset"

In Front of Every Great Photographer

Is

Connectedness

Beauty

Two Soul Sistas – Las Amigas and

"Saturday's Sunset"

One of the benefits of traveling solo is the people you meet along the way. I was adopted by a beautiful family, "The Galvans". I was invited to a sunset ride in a jeep to go take pictures of the flamingos. What an amazing experience! My courage was tested when we had to walk through marshlands barefoot, and it felt like quicksand. Laura and Maximo, two of the most gracious spirits, encouraged me to continue the walk as what I would witness would take my breath away.

"Saturday's Sunset"

Stairway to the Gondola

Burgers anyone? How about Americano style? "Cutie Pie" almost took him home for dessert.

School of Thought: If we never talked to strangers, we might never have any friends.

I hung out with the most beautifully wonderful family who resides in San Diego. Laura, a great new soul-sista friend from Tijuana, her husband Maximo (talented photographer from Italy who took the photos of Laura and I watching the flamingos), and their four beautiful children - Diego, Sebastian, Peter and Marianna. "Galvan Famiglia - Muchas Gracias!"

"Luxuriating Monday"

Dirty minds, it's lip balm

I was born on a Monday, so it was time to have a beachside 90 minute massage, lay in the cabana the entire day and have everything my heart desires brought to me.

Best darn beachside attendant "Alonso"

Sea (See) Birds

There is truth in seeing things from a bird's eye view and being as free as a bird!

"Luxuriating Monday"

The moon, sunset toes and a darling couple (John and Sandy)

"Passionate Tuesday"

Go NACHC Community HealthCorps, DMS live in Colorado and they know about Plan Salud Community Health Center!
GMS   DMS   DMS

The hour boat ride to the whale sharks was extremely rough. There were ten of us on the boat and we all took dramamine before boarding. Two passengers still got sick. Once you're on the boat, there's no turning back

Whale Shark Swim
08.20.13

"Passionate Tuesday"

"Gentle Giants"
Oh My!

Eyes of a Manta Ray

"Passionate Tuesday"

God please keep them safe and please don't let them be harmed or exploited. Amen!

If only I could have touched the Gentle Giants. I would have held them and squeezed them tight or stroked them like they were babies, kittens, puppies or piglets. These photos are a reminder of the joy it brings my heart to swim with them From the looks of this photo, the whale shark looks like that joy is shared.

"Passionate Tuesday"

The first swim was so challenging, the water was extremely choppy and I had a difficult time trying to submerge myself. For the second swim, I almost did not get back in the water. Then I heard Mick's voice saying come on Ma I'm with you. So I put on a life jacket and jumped back in the sea, After the last swim, I could see Mick's face in mine as if his spirit had entered my body.

Nothing like an ice cold Corona, especially now that we are back in the shallow water #IslaMuejeres

On our way back, we were caught in a storm and it whipped our behinds.

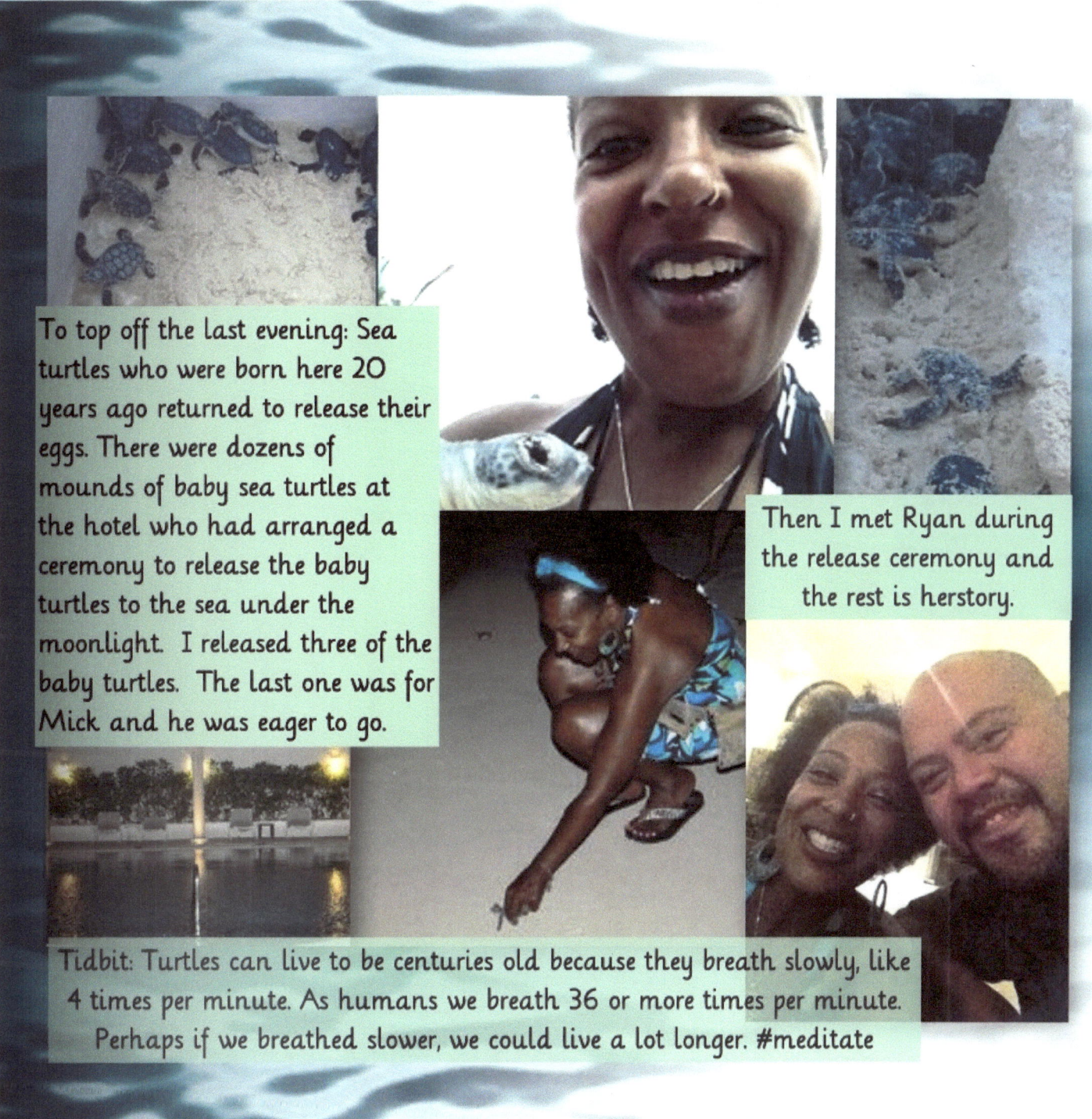

To top off the last evening: Sea turtles who were born here 20 years ago returned to release their eggs. There were dozens of mounds of baby sea turtles at the hotel who had arranged a ceremony to release the baby turtles to the sea under the moonlight. I released three of the baby turtles. The last one was for Mick and he was eager to go.

Then I met Ryan during the release ceremony and the rest is herstory.

Tidbit: Turtles can live to be centuries old because they breath slowly, like 4 times per minute. As humans we breath 36 or more times per minute. Perhaps if we breathed slower, we could live a lot longer. #meditate

What started off as a journey to swim with the whale sharks turned into an adventure and a journey that completely solidified my spirituality. I was really tested for a couple of days in Isla Holbox where I felt like I was in the reality show "Survivor". I learned to enjoy the journey and accept the destination that God set for me, which was greater than I could ever imagine. I meet some of the most wonderful people along the way from different parts of the world (Tijuana, Italy, Australia, Egypt, UK, Croatia, Mexico City and Israel) and the USA (Hawaii, Iowa, Pittsburgh, Oklahoma, New Jersey, Baltimore and Colorado). This trip was about the level of intimacy shared amongst people with kindred spirits or spirits of kindness. There was a connection with them on all levels of joy, pain, laughter, and prayer. This journey was one of the most rewarding yet to come. The people I met along the way: Evon, Giselle, Shellie, John, Sandy, Laura, Maximo, Sebastian, Diego, Ryan, Alonso, Jesus, Jacob, Rebecca, Micah, and Robert. The photos were taken as a reminder of just how much was covered in 8 days. A few of the people were not photographed, but the footprint of our likeness will remain in my heart always. This journey was about how fearless and beautiful the spirit that resides in me has become since the transition of my beautiful son

Smoking tobacco will kill you! Can't be any clearer than this packaging. #WayToGoMexico. Time for me to really consider healthier options.

Return flight: First Class Upgrade. Yeepee!

Not just for me, but one for the spirit of Mick too! #PraiseGod

Adios Mexico!

What I came away with from this Journey:

You know you are in a great place when every animal you see is extremely happy & free

Find laughter everyday even if you are the joke

Stay in different locations when you visit a country

Do something that makes you, not others proud

Australian's eat Kangaroos like American's eat deer

Expect nothing and watch what happens

Always bring a medicine bag fully equipped for an upset stomach, aches, sprains, infections, bm's, heartburn, Mosquitos (spray candles, and bands that make Mosquitos dance).

Don't be afraid to walk in marshlands that feel like quick sand you just might discover Flamingos

If you are looking ahead to the destination, you may lose sight of the journey and all that it has to offer

Share yourself, you didn't invent sin and the pain you share might help someone else

You can use bottle caps for your contact lenses when you're on a remote island

Always get a room with a balcony and a view - the ocean, the sea, the gulf and garden await you

If you don't know the language, try using an object to communicate

Even if the streets have rain water up to your shins, walk barefoot/with flip flops it'll make you stronger

Ride a bus long distance in a foreign country and ask for a dollar, peso, euro, etc. even if it is a seat for your luggage

Some places in the world children walk around butter ball naked.

Tell everyone you love them even if it is with a smile and a wink

Live out loud

If Whale Sharks are gentle and they have a lot of power in weight/size, perhaps as humans we can learn to be kind and gentle with our power

Commercialism and Consumerism are overrated and keep the spirit disconnected from being present

Grasshoppers can be the size of kittens

Dance in the aisle while riding public transportation with music in your ears

Traveling alone takes courage and traveling light is a beautiful thing!

When there are monsoon rains, practice polishing your nails four times

Take photos that deliver messages and they can be a reminder of what you did

Play with yourself it's so invigorating

Eat chocolate just because it's decadent

Find a daily regime that allows you to be still with nature, it is there you can connect with God

Throw kisses at the ground, the sky, the moon, the sun, the wind and the rain

Notes:

Thanks for reading and I hope you enjoyed "Whale Sharks Love Chocolate Too". Please let me know if you enjoyed reading it, as much as I enjoyed putting it together. For further information, details or any comments, please send me an email at grannyd@mac.com This is one of a three part travel series. Part two coming soon "There's Chocolate in the Himalayas"

©2013 Gina M. Smallwood
Please note all photographs are the property of Gina M. Smallwood with the exception of pages 20 and 21 photographed by Massimo Benenti. Do not publish, copy or distribute "Whale Sharks Love Chocolate Too" photo journal in part or whole without prior written consent from the author and that would be me, Gina M. Smallwood.

Travel the world,
It is there you will find a better version of yourself!

This book is dedicated to my late son Kelvin Mikhail. 5% of all net proceeds from the sale of this book will go to WhaleShark conservation and 10% of all net proceeds will go to suicide awareness and prevention.

www.ingramcontent.com/pod-product-compliance
Lightning Source LLC
Chambersburg PA
CBHW060758090426
42736CB00002B/79